what about going out?

warren & ruth peel

CAMERON PRESS
39 Knockbracken Rd, Carryduff, Belfast, BT8 4SF
N. Ireland

Email: bookshop@rpc.org
Web: www.rpc.org

© Warren Peel and Ruth Peel, 2007
All rights reserved. No part of this publication may be reproduced, stored in a retrieval system or transmitted in any form or by any means, electronic or otherwise, without the prior permission of the publishers.

First Published 2007
Reprinted 2014

British Library Cataloguing in Publication Data available

ISBN 978-1-905455-01-0

Unless otherwise stated, quotations from the Bible are from the:

Holy Bible, New International Version © 1973, 1978, 1984 by International Bible Society. Anglicisation copyright © 1979, 1984, 1989. Used by permission of Hodder and Stoughton Limited.

Cover Image: Katinka Kober

Printed by TrimPrint, Armagh

Foreword

This booklet is an expanded version of articles that first appeared in the Messenger magazine. It was a real privilege for us to write them and, after six years of dating and seven years of marriage, it was like taking a refresher course in relationships. We're very conscious of what a hugely important subject this is for Christian young people in 21st century. This is the make or break issue today for many young people—the place where faith proves itself to be true or false. So many who fall away from the gospel do so because they get into a relationship that leads them away from Christ. Please don't be one of them.

Warren and Ruth Peel

Contents

1. Why?   7

2. When?   11

3. Who?   19

4. How?   37

5. How far?   45

6. Who else?   59

7. Where next?   69

> You must unlearn what you have learned.
>
> Yoda - *The Empire Strikes Back*

CHAPTER ONE

why?

Why go out? What is going out about? The first thing you need to do before you go any further in thinking about this question is to flush out of your mind all the brainwashing you have subconsciously been subjected to about going out. As Yoda tells Luke Skywalker in *The Empire Strikes Back*, "You must unlearn what you have learned"—what you've learned about boy/girl relationships from the school playground, from *Friends*, Cool FM and *Titanic*. These are not the places the Christian goes for guidance about going out. Only God's Word can show us the way here: "*Your word* is a lamp to my feet and a light for my path" (Ps 119.105). Not God's Word plus the insights picked up from Albert Square or Summer Bay. What does the world know that our Creator doesn't?

The problem is that, without realising it, so much of what we think about dating may have nothing at all to do with the Bible or Christianity. Loads of our ideas on the subject probably haven't been worked out by careful and prayerful study of Scripture, but "breathed in" passively simply by living in the world. This is always a danger for the believer in every area of life—that we listen more to Chandler, Madonna and Robbie than to Peter, James and Paul.

So what is going out about? The world has very different answers to that question. There are the two extremes, of course. On one hand there are those couples for whom "going out" doesn't mean much more than a snog in the back row of the cinema or at a party. Next Friday night each of them is "going out" with someone different. Then at the other extreme is that couple in your year at school. You know who they are—the whole school knows who they are. They've been going out for a whole month now, and from day one they abandoned all their other friends and seem to live in each other's pockets. They sit together in class. They walk together (hand in hand, of course) between classes and at lunch—and break, and before school, and after school. They are always together and aren't really interested in anyone else. This couple may last a very intense and exclusive six months or one year. Then they will have a big emotional break-up and try to pick up the pieces of their abandoned friendships and schoolwork.

These extremes, sadly, are far from caricatures. We all know couples whose relationships are just like these. And neither kind of relationship is an option for the Christian. But somewhere in between these two poles there are sensible, level-headed couples. Although they're not Christians they do have balanced, healthy relationships with the opposite sex. They don't jump in and out of relationships, but at the same time they don't get obsessive about one another. They are attracted to each another, they agree to have an exclusive friendship—they spend time together and enjoy one another's company. Isn't that what going out is about?

Yes and no. While there are many similarities, perhaps one of the biggest differences between Christians going out and non-Christians going out is that non-Christians tend to treat going out quite casually, not thinking much beyond the next few weeks or months. Christians can't really think that way about relationships. Christians need to take *marriage* into account. Now don't panic! We're *not* saying that you have to marry the person you go out with. We're *not* suggesting that, when you ask someone out, you should also propose marriage to them (you may find if you adopt this approach that you will get quite a few rejections!). We're *not* saying that going out is the same thing as engagement—far from it. Hang on a minute and let us explain.

One of the big mistakes Christian young people make in the whole area of dating is that they treat going out like a bit of a game. It's a kind of hobby to play at—just another one of the things teenagers do. On Saturdays you play rugby or hockey, Tuesday afternoon it's Irish dancing class, Friday nights you see your girlfriend or boyfriend. It's fun to have someone to text, to be part of a couple, to buy and receive presents on special occasions. It's a superficial game—you certainly aren't trying to do anything "heavy" like discover whether or not you may be suited as lifelong partners or anything—you just want someone to go to the school formal with; to be able to say "he's my boyfriend"

You can't separate marriage from going out

so you don't feel left out when everyone else in your class seems to be in a relationship.

But the fact is going out is a stepping stone to marriage. Marriage may (and in most cases *should*) be quite a few years away when you start dating, but, just the same, going out is part of the process that leads to marriage. The chain of dating – engagement – marriage can be broken at the first two stages, but any couple who are now married were once engaged, and before that they were going out. You can't separate marriage from going out—it's the ultimate reason *for* going out.

> "They say that it's better
> to have loved and lost,
> than never to have
> loved at all.
> But if you sit down and
> count the cost of
> all those losses,
> there's no profit at all."

Del Amitri - *You're Gone*

CHAPTER TWO

when?

When is the right time to start going out? Once you get to secondary school? Once you're thirteen, sixteen? After GCSEs? After A-levels? Whenever you want? Whenever someone asks you out? A couple of years ago, one of us was speaking at a church youth group and in the course of the talk asked the children there what they were looking forward to about the Christmas holidays. One of the youngest girls there (who was about eight years old) said the thing she was most excited about was that her boyfriend was coming to visit. Now it may be that her answer was designed more to "impress" the others with how grown-up she was, but just the same there's no doubt that from very early on children feel the pressure of getting a boyfriend or girlfriend.

In our culture, thanks to TV, magazines, and peer pressure at school, young people can be made to feel really quite odd and excluded if they're not going out with someone. And the world so easily infects the church that even at Youth Fellowship, or camp, or church parties, the focus can shift to starting relationships with the opposite sex. But Christians are called by God to be holy in every part of life. "Holy" simply means "set apart" from the world—"different" from the world. Christians don't live their lives by the precepts of *Just 17* or *Neighbours*, but by God's Word. "But all my friends at school are dating!" So what? Ex. 23.2: "Do not follow the crowd in doing wrong." Christians live by different standards—don't just seek a relationship because all your friends are in one.

So what does the Bible have to say about when to go out? When it comes to dating, it's pretty obvious that the culture of the Bible was quite different from ours. Marriages were arranged, and it was perfectly normal for girls to be married and expecting children in their mid-teens. "There you go then!", you say, "In Bible times girls were married by the time they were thirteen or fourteen. Surely no one can object to us just *going out* together if we're that age?" But hold on a minute—remember girls were brought up by their parents from birth to be wives and mothers. By and large they didn't go to school like girls today do—instead they stayed at home with their mothers and learnt

Christians don't live their lives by the precepts of *Just 17* or *Neighbours*

how to cook and keep house. By the time they were eleven or twelve they were probably far better prepared for married life than many young people in their twenties today.

So guidance about going out simply wasn't an issue for the first readers of the Bible, which is why we don't find as much explicit teaching in Scripture on the subject as 21st century readers might like. Does this mean, then, that the Bible is no use to us here? No—to quote the Westminster Confession of Faith: "The whole counsel of God, concerning all things necessary for His own glory, man's salvation, faith, **and life**, is either expressly set down in scripture, or by good and necessary consequence may be deduced from scripture." Everything we need to know about how God wants us to live is in the Bible. Either it will be explicitly spelt out or we'll be able to "deduce it by good and necessary consequence". In other words, if the Bible doesn't say something directly about going out, there will still be biblical principles that apply to this part of life. So what does God's Word have to say to us about when to start a relationship?

Matthew 5.27-30

> "You have heard that it was said, 'Do not commit adultery.' But I tell you that anyone who looks at a woman lustfully has already committed adultery with her in his heart. If your right eye causes you to sin, gouge it out and throw it away. It is better for you to lose one part of your body than for your whole body to be thrown into hell. And if your right hand causes you to sin, cut it off and throw it away. It is better for you to lose one part of your body than for your whole body to go into hell."

This is perhaps the most important biblical principle in this whole area. Jesus says that for citizens of the Kingdom of Heaven purity is so vital that we should sacrifice anything to maintain it. No matter how dear and precious something is to you, if taking it out of your life will help you to be pure, do it. If you start going out with someone quite early on (e.g. thirteen or fourteen), the fact of the matter is that marriage is a long, long way off for you. And as your relationship progresses you'll find yourself

---

Purity is so vital that we should sacrifice anything to maintain it

---

under ever-increasing pressure to misbehave sexually—a pressure that is strong enough because of your hormones, but which is aggravated and intensified a hundred times by films, magazines, advertisements on billboards, your non-Christian friends, and dozens of other influences. Going out while you're still quite young may (we're not suggesting it will in every case) make it hard for you to keep your thoughts and your actions pure. And so Jesus says, "Cut off the right hand." Agonisingly painful though it may be, it may be better for purity's sake not to start a relationship with someone until you're older.

Song of Songs 3.5

"Do not arouse or awaken love until it so desires."

There is debate amongst commentators as to how best to understand this verse, but it certainly includes a warning against plunging into a relationship which demands great maturity before you are ready. Because of the way we are brought up in our culture, the years when we tend to mature and grow up most are between eighteen and twenty-one, simply because this is usually when we either begin work or go to university. It's a time of tremendous change as our personalities, our attitudes and our world-views are shaped, deepened and confirmed.

> Today A is "seeing" B.
> Tomorrow A is "seeing" C, and
> B is "seeing" D.

For this reason there is a great deal of wisdom in not starting a relationship much before this time. Most people simply aren't ready for it—the typical fifteen-year-old is just not mature enough to know how to conduct a Christian relationship.

We want to stress the word "Christian" at the end of the last sentence. We'll expand on this later, but in all of our thinking about this topic we are assuming that the Christian boyfriend/girlfriend relationship is totally different from the non-Christian equivalent. (We're holy remember!) No maturity or wisdom is required to conduct the kind of relationship many of your non-Christian friends jump in and out of. Today A is "seeing" B. Tomorrow A is "seeing" C, and B is "seeing" D. They're not starting a relationship because they want to communicate or get to know one another deeply. The only purpose of the "relationship" (it doesn't even deserve the name) seems to be a few minutes together at lunchtime in some secluded part of the school. That's not the kind of relationship Christians can be involved in. It's a superficial, tacky imitation of the real thing.

The Christian boy/girl relationship is about communicating—learning what the other person is like: what they believe on different issues, what their hopes and ambitions are, what they like and dislike; how they behave in a group, how they relate to and treat other people. To conduct a relationship like this requires a maturity that most (not all) young teenagers tend not to have. So in general it's better not to begin dating early. Emotionally and psychologically, young people in their early to mid-teens are just not ready.

Of course, we all know of couples who started going out in their early teens, who stayed together right throughout school and university, and who have been happily married ever since. But we would suggest that these relationships are very much the exception rather than the rule. In general, "Do not arouse or awaken love until it so desires."

Colossians 3.23

"Whatever you do, work at it with all your heart…"

God calls Christians to work hard and conscientiously at their duties, because in doing so they are actually working for God. If you're a student

At school or university your first responsibility is to study

at school or university, your first responsibility is to study. A thriving social life is not your chief goal at school. Getting into a relationship with someone can become a distraction from this responsibility. Now this is certainly not a reason against going out at school or university, but it is a warning against getting too serious while you're still at school. Some people find it hard once they're in a relationship to stop it taking over their lives.

We know of one case where a couple started going out in 4th year of school and ended up spending all their free time together, both in and out of school. Other friends and activities were put on hold, homework suffered, sport went out the window—all so they could spend more time together. Maturity and self-control are needed to stop that kind of thing happening—a maturity that only tends to develop later.

> **Don't panic. Don't lose your nerve and start a relationship sooner than God says is wise.**

So what is the perfect age to start going out? We'd love to be able to tell you, but since there's no such thing we can't! Human relationships are very far from being a precise science! God has made us all differently. There are some incredibly mature thirteen-year-olds, and some unbelievably immature twenty-five-year-olds! We can't legislate for each person. All we can do is give broad guidelines for each individual to prayerfully consider and apply honestly and submissively to their own case. We wouldn't want anyone reading this to think, "Right—as soon as I'm seventeen I should ask someone out!" We need to be open to God's leading, through his Word and through his providence.

Even in Christian circles there can be a panic to get paired off with someone else as soon as possible. Don't give in to this worldly pressure. We believe in a God who is in control of everything from the orbit of Saturn to the sparrow that falls to the ground—and this God has a plan for his people that involves working everything together for their good. Don't panic. Don't lose your nerve and start a relationship sooner than God says is wise. Pray that he will enable you to be content in your present circumstances, and at the same time pray that he will guide you to the right person at the right time if that's his will for you. If you marry you may have 30, 40, 50 years together. Don't wish away the few years of singleness now when you have so many great opportunities to serve God in a way that married people aren't so free to do. And don't assume that you will necessarily end up getting married. Singleness isn't second-best. God's plan for us is never second-best.

> Many a man in love with a dimple makes the mistake of marrying the whole girl.

Stephen Leacock

CHAPTER THREE

who?

When it comes to dating, it's never too soon to start learning what you're looking for. One of the problems with dating is that too many young people just drift into relationships rather than making a principled decision about whom to go out with. A fellow takes a shine to a girl at a party and decides to ask her out. A girl gets asked out at school one day out of the blue and makes up her mind in the space of about 30 seconds! It's foolish to wait until you are interested in someone or until you get asked out before you start thinking through what the Bible says about whom you should date. There's no time to do it properly then, and it's always much harder once your emotions and hormones are tangled up in a specific person. So get it straight in your mind now, before anyone comes on the scene.

Remember our quotation from the Westminster Confession of Faith? "The whole counsel of God, concerning all things necessary for His own glory, man's salvation, faith, *and life*, is either expressly set down in scripture, or by good and necessary consequence may be deduced from scripture." We may not be able to open the Bible and find the name of the person we should ask out, as the boy who read Isaiah 55.12 thought he had discovered ("You shall go out with joy"), but, as we saw before, the Lord does give us clear principles in his Word to guide us in this whole area.

As we've seen, going out is the first stage of a process that, if unbroken, leads to marriage. Because that's the case *the Lord's commands about whom we may marry apply equally to whom we may go out with*. That means that the first question to ask before you start a relationship with someone is this: "Would God's Word allow me to marry this person?"

i. Right and Wrong Principles
God's Word gives us some crystal clear, non-negotiable principles to help us decide whom to date. They're like four "electric fences" enclosing a square. Anyone on the other side of the fences is out of bounds. Here are the four boundaries God gives: we are free to date and marry anyone who is:

a) a member of the opposite sex
b) not a close blood relative
c) not married already
d) a Christian (1 Corinthians 7.39)
   Here is a clear-cut command from God. A widow is free to marry anyone she wishes. The only restriction on her choice, the only proviso, is that he *must* belong to the Lord. He *has* to be a Christian. There are no two ways about it.

These are clear-cut, right/wrong principles, and if we ignore any one of them we are committing a sin—we are going against the clear teaching of the Word of God. A common question often arises at this point however. Few Christians have any difficulty with (a) to (c), but many do struggle with (d). *Is it always wrong to go out with someone who is not a Christian?*

Now perhaps you don't need to be persuaded that a Christian can't go out with a non-Christian. That's great if that's the case, but you may feel differently when you're suddenly in the position of having to say no to someone you really like. Perhaps you've never found it a struggle turning down a date with that geeky non-Christian with the greasy hair, acne and pierced nose—but what if it's a funny, intelligent, good-looking non-Christian you really look forward to being with? It's vital to be absolutely clear *now*, before the situation arises. Reinforce what you think for when doubts come. Resolve now, ahead of time, that there is simply no way it can happen. It's surprising how many committed, keen Christians waver when they're faced with a boy or girl they really like who isn't a Christian. When their hearts flutter and their legs go weak, suddenly all their principles and convictions go out the window.

Some Christians respond by saying, "But I don't know many Christians—all my friends are non-Christians." If that's the case, they're obviously not spending enough time with Christians. If someone spends all their time hanging out with non-Christian friends and never comes to Youth Fellowship, Camp or other youth events, they only have themselves to blame for not knowing more Christians!

Is it ever right to go out with a non-Christian?

Sometimes you will hear the argument, "Can I not be a good witness to this person if we are going out together? Can I not go out with them to try and win them to Christ?" Perhaps you know cases where a Christian went out with an unbeliever and it led to his or her conversion. Does that not justify the relationship? The only biblical answer to this question is No—a Christian cannot, under any circumstances, go out with a non-Christian. There are several reasons for this:

1. It is faulty reasoning to think that it is right to disobey in order to bring about God's purposes. God *may* (and frequently does) use our disobedience and graciously overrule our sin to accomplish His will (e.g. Genesis 50.20), but that never makes it OK to sin.

2. Emotions can cloud our thinking. Is it *really* because of your desire to see this person become a Christian that you want to go out with them? Are you *honestly* putting their spiritual good first? Or

is it possible that you are attracted to them, want the relationship, and need some way of justifying it to your conscience? Very often this is the motivation behind the question—not wanting to find God's will so much as wanting to bring God's will into line with our will.

3. If you *are* serious about winning that boy or that girl for Jesus—if their spiritual good really is your first concern—then the *worst* thing you can do is to start dating them. All you will do is confuse their motives. Your relationship will make it extremely hard for them to separate their interest in the gospel from their interest in you.

4. More often than not what happens when a Christian starts dating a non-Christian is that the Christian is led away from Christ rather than the other way around. This is why God warns against intimate relationships between Christians and unbelievers. Read 2 Corinthians 6.14-7.1 prayerfully and honestly ask yourself if it is the Lord's will for a Christian to go out with a non-Christian.

5. Let's follow through this scenario a little. Suppose you do start a relationship with a non-Christian. What if after some months (or years?) your boyfriend/girlfriend doesn't become a Christian? What then? You will have become emotionally very close to the other person, making it very hard for you to do the right thing and end the relationship. If you *do* end the relationship, what happens to your original desire to witness to this person? ("I'm splitting up with you because I am a Christian and I can't marry someone who isn't a Christian"—not likely to commend the Christian gospel to them.) *Or* you will disobey the explicit teaching of God's Word by marrying someone who doesn't belong to the Lord (1 Corinthians 7.39). *Or* the other person may say, "OK, I'll become a Christian then." What are the chances of that being a true conversion, born out of repentance and faith?

6. Even to think about going out with a non-Christian reveals a lack of understanding of what a Christian is. Think of how

the Bible speaks about the difference between believers and unbelievers. Christians and non-Christians are on two totally different roads, going in opposite directions to opposite destinies. "What do righteousness and wickedness have in common? Or what fellowship can light have with darkness?…What does a believer have in common with an unbeliever?…Let us purify ourselves from everything that contaminates body and spirit, perfecting holiness out of reverence for God" (2 Corinthians 6.14,15, 7.1). Your whole mindset and way of life are utterly different from that of your non-Christian friends—going out with an unbeliever will only blur that difference. Paul isn't talking here about going out and marriage specifically, but it's a good

---

> **Usually "we have lots in common" really means "we like the same music; we have the same sense of humour; we share a similar taste in films" —utterly superficial similarities**

---

description of those relationships, isn't it? "Yoked together." Christians sometimes say about a non-Christian they want to start dating, "He may not be a Christian, but we have so much in common!" Do you really? The Bible says you're going in opposite directions. Try to look with unbiased eyes at the pairs of opposites described in 2 Corinthians 6.14-16: righteousness and wickedness, light and darkness, Christ and Satan, believer and unbeliever, the temple of God and the temple of idols.

Usually "we have lots in common" really means "we like the same music; we have the same sense of humour; we share a similar taste in films; we are both physically attracted to each other." But these are utterly superficial similarities. God says Christians and non-Christians are poles apart. In every way that

profound, radical differences that affect every significant area of life

really matters they couldn't be more different. The Christian loves God with all his heart, his life revolves around Christ. His chief end is to glorify and enjoy God. The non-Christian hates God and is in rebellion against him. Christians pray and read the Bible every day to learn God's will. The unbeliever isn't remotely interested in God's Word. The Christian battles to resist sin and temptation. The non-Christian is dead in his sins. The Christian is living for the next world. The unbeliever is living for this one. These are not little things—these are profound, radical differences that affect every significant area of life. Christians need to understand how radically different we are from non-Christians. Would you date someone who hated your parents, showed contempt for them, never spoke to them, and wanted nothing to do with them? Of course not. So why would we ever think of doing it to our heavenly Father?

It really couldn't be more clear. Christians may not marry non-Christians or date them. It's a simple matter of doing what the Bible says. Sometimes you hear Christians say, "There's this girl I'm interested in/this guy who's asked me out, but he's not a Christian. But I'm really praying about it." You don't need to pray about it because God has already given his guidance. You can't start that relationship. And if you're in a relationship with someone who isn't a Christian at the moment, then you need to end it immediately. The longer you leave it the harder it will be.

There are also many practical reasons why Christians shouldn't go out with non-Christians, although what we've said so far from Scripture should be enough. Think about this:

Mixed (ie. Christian and non-Christian) marriages and relationships don't work. 99 times out of 100 it's the Christian who gets pulled down. Think of Solomon's tragic example in 1 Kings 11.9-13. The break-up of the kingdom of Israel was directly related to his marriages with unbelievers. We both know of marriages that are wretched and miserable because a Christian married a non-Christian. In the glow of romance before the wedding it really didn't seem all that important, but just a short time into the marriage the Christian realised it just doesn't work. And it's usually the Christian who ends up compromising. He stops going to church; her Bible reading slips; family worship is impossible. How tragic if the person who is meant to be closest to you in the whole world is the one person you can't talk to about the most important things in your life.

It's hard enough to keep going in the Christian life without your husband or wife, your boyfriend or girlfriend pulling you down day after day. Children get very confused in mixed marriages. "Why do we have to go to church when Daddy doesn't?" "Is Mummy going to hell?" Think ahead. It's immature and foolish just to live for the moment—to just enjoy the relationship now without thinking about the future.

The issue couldn't really be much simpler. It's just a matter of doing what God says. The question is will I obey God or will I sin against him? There is no grey area—it really is that simple. This is what it means in practice to say "Jesus is Lord": it means saying, "He rules every part of my life and not just those areas where I find it easy to submit to him. He is Lord over my relationships too, and so I will not start a relationship with anyone he forbids me to date."

ii. **Wise and Foolish Principles**

So far we've looked at clear-cut, right/wrong principles the Bible gives about whom a Christian may go out with and marry. The problem is, of course, that these four principles by themselves will not lead us to the person we should go out with. Think of these conditions as four sides of a square. Anyone outside the boundaries of the square is off limits—but that's still a big square! There are millions and millions of single Christians of the opposite sex who are not blood relatives inside it! Would it be OK to go out with any one of them? We can't say it would be a sin, but there will be many Christians inside the square with whom it may not be wise to begin a relationship.

---

complete freedom inside fixed limits...

If it helps, think of the square as a gymnastics floor. You're not allowed to step outside the square during your routine, but you have complete freedom inside those fixed limits to do what you want. But that doesn't mean that everything you may do is equally sensible. You could hop round the square while patting the top of your head, but you're unlikely to convince the judges of your gymnastic ability! If you want to you can tap dance in the middle of the floor, but don't expect to win any medals. Not everything we may do inside the boundaries is equally wise.

It's this wise/foolish distinction that helps us narrow down the square as we think and pray about whom to go out with. It may not be wrong to go out with a Christian who doesn't speak the same language as you, but given the importance of communication in a relationship, we would have to say it's pretty foolish. It's a silly example, because you're unlikely to ask out someone whose only language is Swahili, but it illustrates the point.

Let's pick a more likely scenario. You're attracted to a Christian who believes it's really important for Christians to speak in tongues, dance in worship, and sing choruses to the accompaniment of an orchestra. Is there much point in starting a relationship if you are convinced we should praise God using the psalms without musical instruments? If you believe God no longer gives the gift of tongues to the church? The relationship can't go anywhere without one of you having a radical change of belief or compromising, so why start it in the first place? This person may be a strong Christian—far closer to Christ than you perhaps, with all kinds of good qualities—but God guides us by sanctified common sense and providence as well as by direct commands. Is he really leading you to this person? It may not be wrong to go out—they're inside the square—but would it be wise?

Weak Christians and backsliding Christians are inside the square, but it would be unwise to go out with one. A newly converted Christian is in

> ...but not everything we may do inside the limits is equally wise

the square, but it would be similarly unwise to jump into a relationship with them before they have had time to get established and grow as a Christian. It may not be wrong, but it's not wise to go out with just anybody in the square, so what we want to do is give you some guidelines to help you narrow down the square.

1. Pray

In James 1.5, God promises to give wisdom to those who lack it, so ask him for it. Ask and believe that he really will guide you. Remember that God is good and kind and that he wants only what is best for you. If your earthly father cares about who you go out with, how much more does your heavenly Father care. He really does care about your life. He knows the number of hairs on your head right now—if he is interested in a trivial little detail like that, he is certainly interested in your relationships. If you want to discover God's will, he is not going to hide it from you. Pray and then be open to his leading.

2. *Have as many boyfriends and girlfriends as possible*

What we mean, of course, is make sure you have lots of friends who are boys and lots of friends who are girls. A romantic relationship should only grow out of friendship. No matter what Hollywood and Top of the Pops say, there is no such thing as love at first sight. Attraction at first sight, yes—but that is no basis to begin a relationship. A relationship like that is selfish because it's only about satisfying feelings. It's completely superficial and has little or nothing to do with the character and personality of the other person. "Love at first sight" is actually pretty insulting when you think about it, because the attraction has nothing whatsoever to do with the things that matter most about a person—their character, their interests, hopes, dreams, the kind of

---

A relationship without friendship will wither and die as soon as the feelings fade

---

person they are. Love at first sight is just about a face and a body, the least important things of all. Proverbs 31.30: "Charm is deceptive and beauty is fleeting; but a woman who fears the Lord is to be praised."

Friendship is the soil out of which romance should grow. A relationship without friendship will wither and die as soon as the feelings fade. Don't go out with someone unless you've got to know them as a friend first. If someone won't wait to get to know you as a friend first, they're not worth getting to know. Christians are people who love one another as they love themselves. When it comes to relationships that means not dating for a week or a month and then breaking up, leaving hurt feelings, bruised emotions and a strained relationship. If you know the person well first, these kinds of emotional disasters will be much less likely.

Having lots of healthy friendships with boys/girls will help you learn how to relate properly to the opposite sex. Paul told Timothy, "Treat younger women as sisters, with absolute purity." Do you, fellows? Girls—do you treat boys at camp or church as brothers? Camp, youth fellowship, youth weekends—they're not for pairing off single young people. They're an opportunity to learn how to relate to one another as brothers and sisters in Christ. Girls, as you develop friendships with boys you'll learn what qualities are important in a guy—and you should discover that it isn't whether or not he has a car and can make a crowded room laugh. Fellows, as you work at being friends with girls, you'll come to realise what qualities really matter and are most attractive in a girl—and they won't be stunning looks and an eagerness to laugh at all your jokes.

The most important thing to discover is whether or not this is someone who is serious about serving God. How can you tell? Well, look at the evidence. Does she go to worship every Sabbath morning and

---

The most important thing to discover is, "Is this person serious about serving God?"

---

evening? Is he actively involved in his youth fellowship? Does she take part in the prayer meeting or the Bible study? Has he ever gone on an outreach team? These things are not conclusive proof that someone's heart is right, but some or all of these things must be present if they're serious about living out their faith. If their relationship with God isn't right, everything else in their life will be off balance. Josh Harris has some sound advice:

> "Look for, and work on becoming, someone who seeks God wholeheartedly, putting him before anything else. Don't worry about impressing the opposite sex. Instead strive to please and glorify God. Along the way you'll catch the attention of people with the same priorities."
> ("I Kissed Dating Goodbye", p192)

3. Get to know one another in all kinds of settings
Pretty much anyone can be dazzling out on a date. A date can be a hopeless way to get to know what a person's really like. In some ways all it will tell you is how good an actor they are! If you are attracted to someone, and they're attracted to you then, of course, you will show yourself off to your best advantage! The guy will be very sensitive

---

At the end of the evening they won't know very much at all about the kind of person the other is

---

and kind and thoughtful—opening doors, paying for everything, and complimenting his date on her appearance. The girl will hang on the boy's every word, laughing in all the right places, and doing whatever he suggests without a hint of complaint. What a perfect relationship! But at the end of the evening they won't know very much at all about the kind of person the other is, because they each have an ulterior motive—they desperately want the other person to like them, so they're on their best behaviour.

If you're going to find out what a boy or girl is really like, you need to be friends with them first and see them in all kinds of different situations when they're not falling over themselves to impress you. A boy may be very attentive to you because he "fancies" you, but how does he treat the other girls at camp? That's a far better indicator of the calibre of person he is. How does he treat the plainer girls? The quiet ones? The less flirty ones? Does he resent talking to them? Does he ignore them, or even treat them with contempt? At a party does he only ask the good-looking girls to dance? Does he willingly play

How does he talk to his mother? How does she treat her little brother?

games with the younger children at the church family night? How does he talk to his mother? Watch him playing games—how does he react when a decision goes against him? When someone fouls him? When someone is better than he is?

That girl may laugh uproariously at your jokes and sit beside you at dinner because she is attracted to you, but how does she treat the less popular fellows? The ones who aren't the stars of the football field? Does she make fun of them? Does she make a face and roll her eyes when she has to sit with one of them instead of being in the popular clique? Is she loyal to her friends and family, or does she slag them off to other people? Does she talk about people behind their backs? Does she stand up for what she believes and stick to her principles, or does she just follow the crowd, and change her behaviour according to who she's with at any given time? How does she deal with pressure at exam time? How does she react to authority? With resentment or with humble and willing obedience? How does that girl treat her little brother? These things are a bit like a window into the future to show how they are likely to treat their husband or wife.

4. Talk about all kinds of stuff
Talk with your boyfriends and girlfriends. You can't get to know someone without talking. Talk about all kinds of stuff. Talk about Christian things. If someone can't talk about spiritual things then don't even consider a relationship with them, because the great purpose of marriage is to help us to love and serve God better. Talk about serious subjects. If someone in your group of friends is never serious, but always turns everything into a joke and is constantly trying to get a laugh, forget about a relationship with them. A clown doesn't make a good husband or wife. At the same time if someone is always deadly serious and has no time for fun and light-heartedness, perhaps that would be an unwise choice of boyfriend or girlfriend too.

Talk one to one; talk in a group. Watch how your boyfriends and girlfriends talk. Do they listen to what others are saying and respect their opinions, or are they always impatient to get their point across.

Have a wish list!

Do you sense she doesn't listen to a word anyone else says and just likes the sound of her own voice? Does he listen to what everyone says, or does he only pay attention to what popular girls say? When he's arguing a point does he get aggressive and lose his temper? Does she belittle someone who disagrees with her, with cutting sarcasm? Jesus says, "Out of the heart the mouth speaks."

5. Have a "wish list"
Perhaps you have a "wish list" for different things—the CDs or DVDs or clothes or whatever that you'd buy if you suddenly had £1000 to

spend. It's your list of ideals. As you do what we've suggested in steps 1-3, you should be drawing up in your mind a "wish list" of the qualities you would want in a husband or wife. But it's essential that your wish list comes from Scripture—that your ideals match up with what God says matter. We want to suggest two phrases that sum up what the Bible says guys and girls should be looking for in a girlfriend or boyfriend.

Girls should be looking for a ***loving leader***. God commands husbands to love their wives just as Christ loved the church and gave himself up for her (fellows, read Ephesians 5.25-29 on your knees and pray that

---

loving leaders & holy helpers, not tyrants & prima donnas

God will make you into that sort of man). The kind of man you want to marry, girls, is someone who will love you with a strong, principled love. Who will put himself out for you no matter what the cost to himself, whether he feels like it or not. Do you know many guys like that? And the husband is given the terrifying responsibility by God of being the leader in the home—the buck stops with him. That means you need a man who can make good and right decisions based on God's Word. You need someone whose opinions and decisions you can respect and submit to. It's possible to be a strong leader and at the same time be utterly insensitive to people's feelings. Girls don't want a jumped-up tyrant full of a sense of his own importance. If she's thinking biblically she will be looking for someone loving and thoughtful who doesn't order her about, but asks for her opinion, seeks her wisdom, values her gifts. If the fellow you're interested in shows no sign whatsoever of being able to do these things, he's not the one for you.

Guys should be looking for a ***holy helper***. God created Eve to be a helper corresponding to Adam's needs. There is nothing remotely inferior about this God-given role—God describes himself in Scripture as *our* helper! This status gives great dignity to women—men can't cope by themselves. They need a helper whose strengths complement their weaknesses. So, fellows, you are looking for a girl who delights in her God-given role—who loves to serve and help others, because it's what her Lord calls her to do. Not someone bossy who resents authority and can't bear to be told what to do. Watch how a girl responds to those in authority over her—her parents, teachers, church leaders. A husband needs a loyal wife—someone he can trust completely, who won't run

> **"Is this the person you want to come home to every night after work?"**

off to gossip about their problems or anyone else's. A good helper must be someone who is disciplined about money and can help you to manage your home responsibly. She (like him) must be self-denying, willing to give of herself in service to others—someone hospitable, who will be able to open her home to welcome friends and strangers alike, regardless of their age, their popularity or personality. A spiritually-minded woman who is able to think for herself—who knows what she believes on important issues and who can challenge you and help you to grow in your understanding. You don't want a wife who is just a "yes woman". A woman of maturity and wisdom—not someone who is petty or vain, superficial or sulky—a little prima donna who needs to be constantly pampered and cossetted.

In all of this it's important to remember God has made us all differently. Relationships are not an exact science. There is no accounting for taste, and personal preference is a big factor in relationships. Different people are attracted to different personalities. Some girls like loud extroverts, others prefer quieter guys. Attraction has its place—it's not just a matter of testing someone against your check list and if he has all the criteria then start a relationship. There is something elusive and mysterious about attraction. Remember though that some characteristics may be cute and endearing for a while as long as you're just dating. Make sure you ask yourself, "Do I want this in a husband or wife?"

In many ways it's only once you're actually in a relationship that you can properly test these things and compare your biblical wish list to your boyfriend or girlfriend. That's the whole purpose of going out—to find out if this guy is the loving leader for you, or if this girl is the holy helper you've been looking for.

> "Lady Churchill's second husband"

Winston Churchill -
*when asked who he would like to be
if he could be someone else*

CHAPTER FOUR

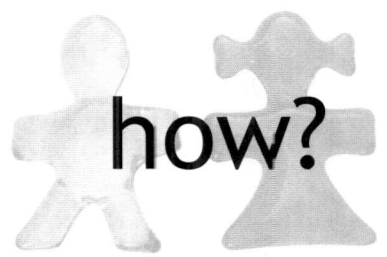

how?

So there's a girl you've been friends with for quite some time now. You met at camp last year and got on well. You've been getting to know her better at the Youth Fellowship weekend, and other places, and the more you find out about her the more you like her. You've heard nothing but good about her from mutual friends. She's a serious-minded Christian—she takes part in discussion groups, and always has something thoughtful to say. She seems to like you—she appears to be glad when you "happen" to end up sitting beside her at a meal or in a meeting. You can talk to each other naturally, and she even liked your joke about the chicken and the elephant! So what now?

There is only so much you can learn about someone by being "just good friends". Sooner or later, if you want to find out whether anything deeper than friendship could come of this relationship, you are going to have to ask the girl out. The purpose of going out is to give you both an opportunity to get to know one another better, as more than just casual friends—to see if you could possibly be marriage material. If you don't have marriage somewhere in mind when you start going out, then you shouldn't be going out. Remember, going out is the first stepping stone to marriage.

Well, how do you start? Well, first-off, the guy should ask the girl out. In marriage the man is given the awesome responsibility by God of being the leader, the head of the home, just as Christ is the head of the church (Ephesians 5.23). You're getting your relationship off on the wrong foot if the boy abdicates his responsibility to lead on the very first opportunity he has to take a lead! That means, guys, that you ask the girl yourself. Don't send a mate to do it for you. Don't write a note. If possible, do it yourself rather than over the phone. That takes courage and leadership—two qualities every girl ought to be looking for in a man. Start as you mean to continue.

She said "Yes"! Great—now what? Well that's what these next few chapters are about. How do you conduct a relationship once you've started one? How much time should you spend together, and what should you do when you are together?

Friendship is a bit like a plant — it doesn't grow overnight

Spending Time Together
How much time depends a lot on circumstances. If you're still at school then, on the basis of the fifth commandment, you should look to your parents to guide you as to how much time you spend together. Family, church and school come first—and if you're spending the right amount of time on each of those (not to mention your existing friendships, about which more later) there won't be a lot of time left over. And anyway it's not a good idea to get too serious too soon.

After you leave school, if you've just started a job, or if you've gone on to university it's harder to keep the balance, because your parents and your professors give you a lot more freedom in the use of your time. You're expected to be mature about what you do with it, but it's still unwise to see too much of each other in the early stages of a relationship. More often than not, a relationship that is very intense from the word "go" causes all kinds of problems. Some of those are physical, as we'll see in the next article, but also emotional. Friendship is a bit like a plant—it doesn't grow naturally overnight. It's a gradual process that takes a lot of careful tending. If you try to force it to grow more quickly than it should you'll end up killing it. Don't rush it. Don't try or expect to become best friends in the first week. You wouldn't spend every moment of every day with anyone else, so don't do it with your new boyfriend or girlfriend. Plan how much time you're going to see each other, and try to keep to that. Restricting your time together forces you to be much more careful and creative in the way you use it, because when it's scarce and precious you won't want to waste a single second of it.

So how should you use your time? At the risk of sounding repetitive, remember that the great purpose of going out is to get to know one another better. To discover more about each other's personality and character. So plan your time together around this great purpose. If you only ever go to the cinema, or watch a video, or go to a concert, you'll be bang up to date with pop culture, but you'll flop when it comes to understanding each other's character! "Don't stress yourself out trying

---

The great purpose of going out is to get to know one another better... plan your time together around this great purpose

---

to orchestrate incredibly entertaining or romantic dates. Relax and enjoy each other's company... The strategic question to keep in mind is: How can you let each other see the 'real you"? (Joshua Harris, Boy Meets Girl) If you find that you can't sustain a relationship by "just" talking, and that you need lots of distractions and entertainment to fill up the space, you're probably not well suited for marriage.

Communicate
The best way to get to know someone is to talk with them. So however you spend your time, make sure you can talk together lots while you're doing it. We have found that going for a walk together is one of the

easiest ways to talk, but find what works for you. Communication is two-way. A relationship shouldn't be one person doing all the talking and the other doing all the listening (or ignoring!). Both of you need to talk and share your thoughts and feelings. That's especially important to realise if one of you is naturally quite talkative and the other is quieter. The temptation for Little Miss Chatterbox is to chatter all the more because she has a quiet boyfriend, while Mr Quiet is happy to keep quiet and let his girlfriend chat happily away.

Make sure you talk about all kinds of stuff. This is what we suggested you do before going out as well, but once you start going out you keep doing the same things—it's just that you have more opportunities to do them to a greater degree. So now that you're going out you can open up a lot more about your hopes and ambitions for the future. You can

---

Talk seriously. Some couples never stop talking; they just never say anything!

---

talk more freely now about your thoughts on marriage, family, work, church, money, and so on. Talk seriously. Some couples never stop talking; they just never say anything! Don't shy away from subjects you disagree on. It may be easier to leave them alone, but you won't progress your relationship very much. Of course, you won't agree with each other on every single thing—so you need to learn how to deal with differences of opinion without arguing and losing your temper. Learn to listen to what each other is really saying and not just what you think they're saying or expect them to say. The sooner you develop this skill in your relationship the better! Learn to respect each other's point of view, even if you don't agree with it—and if you can't do that then frankly you'd better call it quits now.

Talk about your feelings. (Don't stop reading, men!) That may be hard work if you're quite a reserved person, or even if you're just a typical bloke, but as you get to know one another better you should open up and share your feelings more. Going out is a stepping stone to marriage. Husbands and wives need to talk about these kinds of things and, if you don't talk about them when you're going out, how can you know you'll be able to talk about them after you're married?

Learn to listen—especially if you're not a naturally good listener. Don't assume you know what the other is thinking or saying. Look each other in the eye and concentrate on what the other is saying. We all need to work at being better listeners. It may even be that from time to time what your boyfriend or girlfriend is saying may not actually interest you all that much (and if you find this happens a lot, perhaps you should rethink your relationship!), but make sure you listen. No-one is constantly sparkling, and in marriage there will be times when it doesn't come easily to hang on every word the other speaks. Many of the problems in every relationship arise when one or both parties don't listen properly—they hear what they want to hear or what they think they hear. It's a recipe for disaster.

> Don and Susan got married after two years of dating, only to discover how little they had actually communicated with each other beforehand. "Marriage was a huge wake-up call for us," Don says. "We didn't really know each other that well because our communication had been so superficial... Our dating was mostly focused on fun activities. We hardly ever talked about what we felt or believed." We men should assume the responsibility of initiating meaningful communication in our relationships. Don't just plan activities, plan conversations. When Shannon and I began our courtship, I was bursting with questions for her. I wanted to know everything I could about this girl. What did she love? What did she hate? What made her laugh? What made her sad? What kind of songs did she sing when no one was around? What did

she order at an Italian restaurant? What was one of her mother's traits she most admired? Who influenced her most growing up? (Joshua Harris, *Boy Meets Girl*)

Most of all, try to encourage each other to grow spiritually. Get into the practice of praying together and talking about spiritual issues. It may seem awkward or difficult at first, but the more you do it, the more natural it will become. Start as you mean to continue. If you can't talk about what should be at the centre of both of your lives and more important to you than anything else, there is something wrong. Talk about what you learned in your Quiet Time this morning, how you've been challenged or encouraged by this week's sermon, what's going on in your church. Share prayer points with each other and pray them through every day. Talk about Christian books you've read and exchange them. Read the same book separately and talk about it when you're together. Men, it's your responsibility to lead in all areas of your relationship, but especially in this one. You're the one who will be answerable to God for having family worship in your home—you should be taking the lead in talking about spiritual things.

Participate
Hopefully you will have some common interests that you can enjoy together as a couple—perhaps something that brought you together in the first place. It's good to develop these and look for other things you can enjoy doing together. Sitting around the house with nothing much to do doesn't make for a stimulating relationship with anyone, and, when it's your boyfriend or girlfriend, you're putting yourself in the path of temptation.

It may be that your boyfriend's hobby doesn't do much for you personally. Cross-country running, chess, or golf may not be very high up on your list of fun things to do on a Friday night. And perhaps you don't quite share your girlfriend's passion for classical concerts, cross-stitching or craft fairs. But if you're going to work at a relationship with this person, then their interests and loves should be important to you. Take an interest in what they do. Ask them about it—find out why they enjoy it so much. Go with them. Who knows—you may end up becoming a cross-stitching cross-country enthusiast yourself! Love is not about what the other person can do for us—it's about what we are prepared to do for the other person. When you love someone, you accept the whole person—all their interests and hobbies and eccentricities.

Use your time together creatively and constructively. Make it serve your goal in going out—to get to know one another better and better as people. If you keep this purpose central it will help keep your relationship on the right track and guard against one of the greatest dangers in dating—sexual sin.

> **When you love someone, you accept the whole person—all their interests and hobbies and eccentricities**

> "I just thought you guys were having sex.
> I didn't know you were in love!"

Phoebe - *Friends*

CHAPTER FIVE

how far?

There is a temptation for anyone who reads a book or a series of articles about boy/girl relationships to jump ahead to the part that deals with sex. Ask yourself if, even subconsciously, you have been anticipating this particular topic more than any of the others. Have you skipped ahead to read this bit first? Why should that be the case? There may be a number of reasons. Perhaps this is an area of Christian living where you really struggle and particularly need help. That's quite understandable, given the world's attitude to sex. But it's possible to have less good motives in reading up on this.

Purity

There's something in us (the Bible calls it "the flesh") that takes an unwholesome delight in thinking about sexual sin. Somehow the fact that we're discussing ways of keeping ourselves sexually pure seems to make it OK to talk about things that we spend the rest of our time trying not to think about. We need to be on the alert to the subtlety of the flesh, and the skill of the Devil in tempting us. Robert Murray M'Cheyne, a godly minister of the 19th century said, "I find that speaking of some sins defiles my mind and leads me into temptation." We need to be careful that we don't discuss these things in a way that actually stirs up thoughts and desires that are harmful. Sin is more deadly than radioactive poison, because even just talking about—even just thinking about it—can hurt us. Handle with extreme care.

Or it may be that we eagerly devour all kinds of books and articles on this subject because deep down we're hoping for a different answer each time. We're hoping each time that this writer, this speaker is going to say it's OK to do just a little bit more physically, or help us to justify to our consciences what we're already doing. Many who have dealt with this subject have given useful "rules of thumb" for how a Christian couple should behave physically in a relationship. "Don't touch what you haven't got"; "Four on the floor" (i.e. four feet on the floor at all times). Some divide physical contact up into categories ranging from no touching at all, through light petting, heavy petting, and so on up to sexual intercourse. They then suggest drawing a line at a particular category. Others have argued that the purity of a kiss is proportionate to the number of seconds it lasts!

The problem with giving guidelines and rules like this is that if our *heart attitude* is not right then we will find a way round them so that we can do what we want while still keeping the letter of the law. So we persuade our conscience that what we're doing is still OK because we've got four feet on the floor, even though we're completely missing the whole point of the rule. Suppose you decide that all you're going to do with your boyfriend/girlfriend is to give each other a hug. Well and

> **The problem with rules is that if our heart is not right we'll find a way round them**

good—but there's a way of hugging that is innocent and chaste, and then there's a way of taking your girlfriend in your arms and holding her and pressing tight against each other that is extremely sensual and designed to arouse sexual desire. You see the problem with rules? They don't protect us against our hearts if our hearts aren't right.

And that's really the crucial point we want to make here. It's your heart that is the key thing. If you don't really want to keep yourself sexually pure in your thoughts and actions then you won't, no matter how many rules and guidelines you set yourself. You'll twist them and stretch them to fit what your heart wants. Your heart is quoting the famous phrase of Augustine: "Lord, make me pure, but not yet."

On the other hand, if a couple is really serious about purity then in a sense they don't really need any rules, because they will do whatever it takes to keep themselves pure. So that's the issue for all of us. Do you want to keep yourself pure as the Lord calls you to be? Then the question is not, "How far can we go?" but "How can we make sure we keep our relationship pure?"

> **"Imagine your body is made of gunpowder… How careful you'll be then to keep away from sparks."**

Here's a helpful illustration taken from the Puritan theologian John Owen. He said, "Imagine your body is made of gunpowder. One tiny spark will ignite it and blow it to smithereens. How careful you'll be then to keep away from sparks." You won't be asking, "How close can I get to a spark without actually catching fire?" You'll be saying, "I don't want to come within a hundred miles of the tiniest spark—my life depends on staying as far away from sparks as possible." Are you playing with fire in your relationship at the moment?

How to stay away from sparks
(By the way, if you're not in a relationship with anyone at the moment, don't switch off or skim this bit. These biblical guidelines apply to all Christians, regardless of their dating status.)

Watch what you watch
Males are turned on by what they see. That is well known and easy to understand, but it often seems that Christian girls simply haven't grasped this. If you know that fellows struggle to control their thoughts, why would you wear a top that is honestly too tight or too low or reveals half your midriff? Girls, you need to show compassion and sensitivity to your brothers in Christ here, because most of us are very weak. We need you to help us. This summer's fashion may be plunging necklines,

---

They're made of gunpowder... and by dressing provocatively you're waving a lighted match

---

but purity matters more to God than trendiness. This point has been made countless times, but many of you girls simply haven't taken it on board. Perhaps it's just naivety, or perhaps it's more serious than that, but you don't seem to be taking seriously the damage you can do by the way you dress. Please show love to your brothers by being careful about what you wear. They're made of gunpowder, and by dressing in a provocative way you're waving a lighted match under their noses.

Men, because God has made you to be stimulated primarily by sight, you need to be so careful about what you let your eyes see. Job was a righteous man, but he had to say, "I have made a covenant with my eyes not to look lustfully at a girl." We need to make a covenant with our eyes that we simply will not look at what will stimulate a desire we cannot lawfully satisfy. That will mean not watching certain TV programmes or films. It may mean being accountable to someone about the internet sites we visit. It may mean not watching certain music videos. It will mean not reading certain books or magazines. It will mean we are disciplined about where we let our eyes linger in the street or restaurant. Jesus says, "If your eye causes you to sin, pluck it out and cast it off." No matter how extreme the cure, do whatever it takes to keep yourself pure. You're made of gunpowder, and what you see can so easily light the fuse.

Don't be so touchy
Something we've noticed in our own experience at Camp, church weekends and the like is that some guys and girls have a bad habit of snuggling up together. A girl sits on a boy's knee or rests her head on his shoulder while he puts his arm round her. Or a girl stands behind a fellow and massages his shoulders. You all know the kind of thing we're talking about. Innocent? Perhaps in theory. But if you want to stay away from sparks it's not sensible. Even a very small touch can be enough to stir impure desires in a guy. Meanwhile the danger for the girl is to read too much into an apparently "innocent" action. The

... cruel and selfish...

temptation for girls in general is not so much physical but emotional. A girl likes the romance of feeling secure and protected and cosy when a guy sits with his arm round her. To awaken desires in someone that we have no ability to satisfy is not a loving way to behave towards one another as brothers and sisters—it's cruel and selfish.

How far to go when going out
It's important to understand that things don't suddenly change once you start going out with someone. In the world they do. As soon as your non-Christian friends start going out they regard it as their right to kiss each other passionately and much more besides. For many that is the only reason for going out at all. But the world doesn't set the standard for Christians—God does.

> "It is God's will that you should be sanctified: that you should cut yourselves off from sexual immorality; [4]that

each of you should learn to control his own body in a way that is holy and honourable, ⁵not in passionate lust like the heathen, who do not know God; ⁶and that in this matter no-one should wrong his brother or take advantage of him. The Lord will punish men for all such sins…⁷For God did not call us to be impure but to live a holy life. ⁸Therefore he who rejects this instruction does not reject man but God, who gives you His Holy Spirit" (1 Thessalonians 4.3-8).

There are two verbs in v6 of this passage that are especially relevant to Christians in their relationships. Paul says no one should "wrong his brother". The verb describes stepping over the mark, trespassing on private property. Until you are married your boyfriend or girlfriend's body doesn't belong to you, so if you misbehave sexually you are trespassing on private property. More than that, your boyfriend or girlfriend doesn't even own their body—1 Corinthians 6.19-20 makes it clear that you're trespassing on what belongs to the Lord. The other verb is "take advantage of him". This word describes a greedy desire for something that is more than our fair share, something more than what we're entitled to. That's a good description of sexual misconduct.

> **God doesn't command us to live like this to make us miserable but to make us happy**

It's selfishly taking more than we have a right to, simply to gratify our wants and desires. We're "taking advantage" of the other person and using them. If you haven't pledged yourselves to each other publicly in marriage, then hands off—you have no right to touch the other person.

Now that simply isn't how the world thinks. For most of your non-Christian friends this teaching is from another planet. And, of course, in a sense, it is. It comes from heaven—have another look at v8 above. If you decide to ignore this teaching it's not any human advice you're rejecting. It's not the apostle Paul you're ignoring. You're rejecting the word of Almighty God Himself. This is not the ranting of a repressed, prudish killjoy—they are God's commands that bring holiness, happiness and freedom. This point

God is not a cosmic killjoy

is often lost in discussions of sexual purity, that God's ways are best. God doesn't command us to live like this to make us miserable but to make us happy. Remember, sex was invented by God to be enjoyed by us—but only when we follow the Maker's instructions. Sexual sin brings temporary bursts of pleasure, but more than anything else guilt and broken hearts. Josh McDowell puts it this way in "Why Wait?",

> "Not only does God know us intimately, but he also loves us dearly…Whenever God does something, he does it out of love for us… Behind every negative commandment in the Bible are two positive principles: One is to protect us; the other is to provide for us. In other words, when God says, 'You shall not commit adultery,' he is not being a cosmic killjoy. He is a cosmic lovejoy. He is saying, 'I don't want you to do something that will bring you and others pain; I have better things planned for you.'"

What is the result of sexual sin? "You will lose your honour and hand over to merciless people everything you have achieved in life. Strangers will obtain your wealth, and someone else will enjoy the fruit of your labour. Afterward you will groan in anguish when disease consumes your body" (Proverbs 5.9-11, NLT). Exaggeration? Not when you look beyond those brief moments of pleasure that lust delivers. Listen to Josh Harris:

Ask Michelle, a girl I met at a Christian bookstore in Phoenix. For twenty-two years she saved her virginity for her future husband. She was working as a model when she met an attractive man who was determined to deflower her. She toyed with him, loving the attention. Then one day on his apartment couch she gave in to his advances. Only once. Less than an hour of stolen pleasure. Now he's gone, and she's a single mom struggling to care for her fatherless two-year old daughter.

The Bible isn't just being dramatic when it says that you'll 'groan in anguish when disease consumes your body.' Just ask the missionary in Asia that a pastor told me about. He was a virgin in his early thirties and two months away from getting married. One night, inflamed by lust and tired of resisting temptation, he made his way to the

Too many people, especially fellows, just don't want to be pure

red-light district of the city and the bed of a prostitute. Only once. Just fifteen minutes in a dark, dingy room—a moment of indulgence in years of work for God. But he left infected with AIDS. Two months later he unwittingly infected the bride who had waited so patiently for him. He groans in anguish at the disease that now wracks both of their bodies.

If these examples seem extreme, just look into the eyes of the countless men and women who have neither illegitimate children nor disease, but who are scarred

> with shame and regret… Talk to the married couples who sinned together before marriage and who have spent years recovering from the bitterness and distrust it sowed in their relationship. ("Boy Meets Girl," p147)

"So you're saying we can't do anything? We can't touch each other? We can't hold hands, or hug, or give each other a quick peck on the cheek?" As we said at the beginning, we're not going to say, "It's OK to do x", because no matter how "tame" x is there may be a way of doing it that is perfectly innocent and holy and honourable, and there will be a way of doing it that is immoral and driven by lust. The thing that makes the difference is the attitude of your heart, so that's what we want to urge you to get right. If your heart is right then if you give each other a hug you'll make sure it's brief and not designed to arouse. If your heart is wrong then if you hug it will be lingering and up close, and you'll use that contact to indulge your physical desires. So we're not going to say "a, b and c" are OK, but "x, y and z" are out of the question. Instead ask yourselves honestly, "How can we make sure we cut ourselves off from sexual immorality?" and if you honestly want to be pure, there won't really be many grey areas about what you should and shouldn't do. Let's face it; we know when we're doing something that is arousing us, or in order to arouse the other person. If our heart's desire is for purity we'll say, "Sorry, but we can't do this."

The root problem is that too many people, especially fellows, just don't want to be pure. What they need is not more rules and guidelines but a change of heart. And the wonderful good news for anyone struggling in this area is that if you're a Christian God is able to give you that. In v8 of the 1 Thessalonians passage above God is described as the one who gives us his Holy Spirit. The word "holy" is strongly emphasised in the original language—we can be holy as God calls us to be because his Holy Spirit lives in our hearts. He gives the power to grow in holiness.

Things to do
Practically speaking there is a number of things you can do to help avoid temptation.

- Set your standards in the cold light of day, from Scripture, and not while you're both cuddled up on the sofa, alone in the house for the evening, with romantic music playing and the lights turned down low. Then having set your standards, stick to them ruthlessly. They may be the best, purest and strictest standards in the world, but if you don't actually live by them they are completely worthless. It's like those students who are so good at drawing up revision timetables that require them to work ten hours a day, but who never actually follow their timetable and do any revision.

- Pray. "The prayer of a righteous man is powerful and effective." In ourselves we don't have the strength to resist sexual temptation, any more than any other temptation. But we can do all things through him who gives us strength (Philippians 4.13). Pray yourself before you go out to see your boyfriend/girlfriend. Here's one teenager's prayer: "Dear Lord, trusting you for strength, I promise to keep myself pure for the person I am to marry, by abstaining from sex and from any other physical expressions that do not honour you." Pray together. Start and end your dates with prayer. "Starting off the date with prayer will give you the opportunity to commit your date to the Lord together and ask His guidance on it. Knowing that you will be ending the date in prayer will give greater motivation to keep your words and actions such that you won't need to be ashamed before God." ("Why Wait?" Josh McDowell, p364)

- "Brad continually tried to wear down his girlfriend, Allison, with requests for 'just one kiss,' even though they had agreed to save that for engagement. We should never expect the other person to be the strong one and force them to bear the weight of temptation. How unloving!" (Boy Meets Girl, p153)

Stay out of each other's bedrooms

- Don't spend long periods of time alone when you're unlikely to be disturbed. Stay out of each other's bedrooms. If one of you has a car, don't park in secluded spots and sit in it together. Students away from home need to be especially careful about spending time in each other's rooms, particularly when it may be normal practice amongst your non-Christian friends for girlfriends and boyfriends to spend the night.

Mark the occasions when you have fallen, and avoid the occasion as much as the sin itself

- Of course, you need time by yourselves to talk and get to know each other better and better. Go for walks—the only thing you can realistically do while you're walking is talk. When you are by yourselves at home, don't sit draped over each other on the sofa. If you can't control your hands, find something for them to do. Work at a hobby together that enables you to talk at the same time.

- Be careful what you talk about. It's not helpful to talk too much about physical temptation, or to go into lurid details about things that arouse you and tempt you.

- Never underestimate the power of temptation or the weakness of your own heart. Don't think, "I would never do such and such a thing." If you think you are standing firm, be careful that you don't fall! (1 Corinthians 10.12)

- Listen to Robert Murray M'Cheyne: "I ought to mark strictly the occasions when I have fallen, and avoid the occasion as much as the sin itself." That's helpful advice in the whole area of sexual purity. If you find you just can't be alone as a couple in private without falling into sin, don't be alone in private. Sounds drastic? Yes, but that's exactly what Jesus prescribes in Matthew 5.29-30: no matter how radical the remedy, no matter how much it hurts, if that's what it takes to keep yourself pure, do it.

- Unless you're going away as part of a group of friends, the first holiday you go on together should be your honeymoon. Going away alone together is utterly foolish—it is putting yourselves in the way of temptation and asking for trouble.

- Always remember that however sure you both may be now that you are meant for each other, your relationship may not end in marriage. Don't give yourselves any cause for regret—you want to be able to look each other in the face if you break up.

You want to be able to look each other in the face if you break up

We know very well that the things we've said here sound extreme. That's partly because the world's standards are so lax, but it's mainly because God is extreme when it comes to sexual purity. If your eye causes you to sin, gouge it out and throw it away. Are you going to tell Jesus he was over the top? "But among you there must not be **even a hint** of sexual immorality… because this is improper for God's holy people" (Ephesians 5.3). "**Flee** from sexual immorality… You are not your own; you were bought at a price. Therefore honour God with your body" (1 Corinthians 6.18-20). We could multiply quotations, but you see the point. If you're not striving with all your might for purity, you're out of step with God.

Sexual purity is where the battle is raging for most young people today. Perhaps never before in human history has it been so difficult to keep our hearts pure. Sex outside marriage has become completely normal—there is now no stigma attached to it by society in any way. Instead there is a stigma attached to those who want to keep themselves for their husband or wife on their wedding night. We are bombarded every day with images and ideas in the media designed to make us lust. The world, the flesh and the Devil are working together to bring us down. Many young people give up on Christianity, not because they don't believe the Bible or don't accept they need to be saved from hell, but because they are enticed away by the excitement of sexual immorality. Don't open the door even a little. Remember if you're made of gunpowder even the tiniest spark can kill you.

God is extreme when it comes to sexual purity... Are you going to tell Jesus he was over the top?

> "A great marriage is not when the 'perfect couple' comes together. It is when an imperfect couple learns to enjoy their differences."

Dave Meurer - *Daze of Our Wives*

CHAPTER SIX

who else?

Two's company, but three's allowed (or four, or five, or six…). In this chapter we want to deal with another pitfall in dating—being too exclusive. Becoming too "wrapped up" in each other, too "couply", "living in each other's pockets". Whatever you call it, it's a sign of an unhealthy relationship. Let's look at a couple of case studies first, to be sure we all understand what we're talking about here. They're both taken from Joshua Harris's book I Kissed Dating Goodbye.

> While Garreth and Jenny were dating, they didn't need anyone else. Since it meant spending time with Jenny, Garreth had no problem giving up Wednesday night Bible study with the guys. Jenny didn't think twice about how little she talked to her younger sister and mother now that she was dating Garreth. Nor did she realise that, when she did talk to them, she always started her sentences with, "Garreth this…" and "Garreth said such and such…". Without intending to, both had foolishly and selfishly cut themselves off from other relationships… When Garreth and Jenny mutually decided to stop dating, they were surprised to find their other friendships in disrepair. It's not that their other friends didn't like them; they hardly knew them anymore. Neither had invested any time or effort in maintaining these friendships while they concentrated on their dating relationship.

Sarah and Philip are both seniors in high school and have gone out with each other for six months. Their relationship has reached a fairly serious level. In fact, for all intents and purposes, they might as well be married. They rarely do anything apart—they monopolise each other's weekends, drive each other's cars, and know each other's families almost as well as their own... And in reality, if they are like most high school couples, each of them will probably marry someone else.

Get the picture? It's a fairly common scenario, isn't it? Perhaps you have friends who are in relationships like this at the moment. Or perhaps you even recognise yourself here. But so what? "What if my relationship is like that? What's the big deal? Haven't you been telling us all along not to go out casually? That it's a serious thing to date? Now you're saying we're too serious? Make up your minds!" But taking a relationship seriously doesn't mean behaving as though you're already married. There are a number of dangers to be aware of.

Taking a good thing and making it the ultimate thing—that's idolatry

Most important of all, be aware that the closer things are to our hearts, the greater the danger of them becoming idols in our lives. Throughout our lives we need to beware of putting any other gods before the Lord. Things and people that are important to us can so easily usurp God's place in our hearts. For parents it might be their children. For the accomplished pianist it might be music. For the 1st XV player it might be sport. For the competent and skilful architect or the dedicated farmer it might be work. Perhaps for you it's your boyfriend or girlfriend. Are they becoming an idol to you? Do you devote your best energies to serving your relationship—the better part of your time and money? Do your thoughts constantly dwell on his voice or her face? Does your boyfriend/girlfriend receive greater devotion from you than your God and Saviour? Then there's an idol that needs to be smashed.

Being too wrapped up in your relationship siphons off time and energy that needs to be dished out over a number of vital areas. You have all kinds of responsibilities in your life and, like it or not, your boyfriend/girlfriend doesn't top the chart.

1. ***An unhealthy relationship steals commitment to church.*** A line of a poem by G. Studdert Kennedy sums up this danger: "I cannot get to Jesus for the glory of her hair." Instead of going to the Youth Fellowship or the midweek meeting, you're with your girlfriend/boyfriend. There's no time for Mission Teams or the like in the summer (unless you're going together of course), because every second of the holidays needs to be spent together. Be careful—church services and meetings are not dates. Don't fall into the habit of always going to one or other of your congregations

> *"I cannot get to Jesus for the glory of her hair"*

together (or if you belong to the same congregation, always sitting together), or only going to a meeting if the other is going too. God has placed you in a particular place at a particular time as a single person—make sure you serve him wholeheartedly where you are. Don't rob your own church family of your contribution and fellowship and service because you're always running off to your boyfriend's or girlfriend's church.

2. ***An unhealthy relationship steals contentment with your family.*** Until you're married you and your boyfriend/girlfriend

are not a family. So don't behave as though you are. Elisabeth Elliot: "Unless a man is prepared to ask a woman to be his wife, what right has he to claim her exclusive attention? Unless she has been asked to marry him, why would a sensible woman promise any man her exclusive attention?" Your *family* is your family. That may seem obvious, but you wouldn't know it to look at some couples. The danger with getting too intense in going out is that you are no longer happy to spend time with mum and dad, with your brothers and sisters. Instead you're counting down the days and hours until you can be with *Him* or *Her* again. That's not how it's meant to be. Until you get married your family should hold first place in your affections. If this isn't the case for you, either you are becoming obsessive about your boyfriend/girlfriend, or there is something wrong with your relationship with your family that by God's grace you need to deal with. Make the most of the time you have with your family at this stage in your life—it'll pass before you know it, so enjoy it to the max while it lasts. Don't make your brothers and sisters feel awkward in their own home and family because you always have to have your boyfriend/girlfriend round.

3. ***An unhealthy relationship poisons your companionship with your friends.*** No one likes to be used, but when a guy and girl get obsessive about being together they all too often end up using their other friends. They only want them when their boyfriend/

> **It's as if their friends have "in case of emergency" written across their foreheads!**

girlfriend isn't available. It's as if their friends have "in case of emergency" written across their foreheads! Or if this couple doesn't ignore their friends they make them feel left out, excluded—big green gooseberries. Couples who are all over each other (whether physically or not) when they're with a group of friends are too selfish and self-absorbed to realise how uncomfortable and awkward they are making their friends feel—especially if some of their friends don't happen to be in a relationship with anyone. Jesus says the Christian treats others as he or she would like to be treated. Don't be insensitive to their feelings. Camp, youth group, and outreach teams are not dates. The purpose of going is not to have a cosy time with your boyfriend/girlfriend but to focus on God and enjoy fellowship with *everyone*.

4. ***An unhealthy relationship disrupts your concentration at school/college.*** Jack was a good student and a valuable member of the senior hockey team. Shirley was a keen actress and never missed a school play. Her schoolwork was always consistently good. When Jack and Shirley started going out together everything changed. There just weren't enough hours in the day to see each other, so Shirley started skipping rehearsals after school while Jack cut hockey training so they could be together. They skimped on homework so they could talk on the phone or write long "love" letters to each other. Their marks suffered and they progressively lost interest in everything except each other. But they were in "love", so what else mattered?

But that's exactly the fallacy—this kind of relationship isn't love at all. It's the very opposite of love. "Love is not self-seeking" (1 Corinthians 13.5). In other words, it wants what is best for the other person, not what will make me feel good. The kind of relationship we've been talking about isn't based on love, but selfishness. That's evident in what comes out of a relationship where a couple are too wrapped up in themselves: idolatry, obsession, insecurity, possessiveness, suspicion, envy, ill-feeling amongst friends, and more besides. Far from being secure in each other's love, the couple can't handle not being together, can't handle being apart in a group, don't trust each other to be with anyone else at all, and so it goes on in a downward spiral. It doesn't sound very Christian, does it? It isn't. If your relationship is going down this road at the moment then it's time to fix it or end it.

a word to parents…

May we say a word to parents at this point? We mustn't abdicate our God-given responsibility in this whole area. Let's not be brainwashed by TV and film into thinking that our teenager's love life is somehow outside the bounds of our control, that it's "none of our business", that we "mustn't interfere". God has charged us with protecting and guiding our children from harm in all its forms—this included.

But let's look at the whole thing from a more positive angle now. We've seen the pitfalls and their consequences. What's the answer? Obviously as you progress in a relationship you'll grow closer. Your affection for each other will deepen. You'll share a great deal together and come to understand and know each other really well (if you don't, you're doing something wrong!). The temptation will be to phase out the rest of the world. How do you avoid that? Here are some practical guidelines to help keep things in perspective:

- Make spending time with your family a priority every week. Whoever else you see, make sure you see them. Some families have a certain night of the week when everyone stays in and plays games/watches a film together—that certainly makes it easier. The Lord's Day is of course tailor-made by God to give us time together as families. If you're away from home during the week, or during term-time, then it's all the more important that you set aside time when you're home to be with your family. Don't resent this time—it will pass very quickly. Look forward to it; value it. Don't mope and pine in the corner. Take part cheerfully in whatever's happening. Don't give everyone the impression you're doing them a huge favour by staying in—that's it's a painful sacrifice to give up a night when you could be seeing your boyfriend/girlfriend.

- Talk to your family—both your parents and your brothers and sisters. Don't just drop them now that you have someone else close to talk to. Don't let your new relationship drive a wedge between you and your family.

- Talk to your parents about your relationship. It should be them you go to for advice about boys/girls first—not your best mate. Your parents (believe it or not!) are a lot wiser than your teenage friends! They have successfully come through courtship and have been learning about marriage for a long time. They know a thing or two

Keep your perspective, your family, your friends

about relationships! What is God's number one commandment to do with other people? Honour your father and mother—that means listen respectfully and obey what they say. Until you set up your own home you are under their direct authority (and remember there's no age limit on this commandment—you don't stop honouring your parents after you're 21—you should always take their advice very very seriously.)

- Bring your boyfriend/girlfriend into your family context. "Meeting the folks" shouldn't be the absolute last step in a relationship that it is in films. It will give your parents a chance to get to know him/her, to see how he/she interacts with the rest of the family, to see what kind of a person they are so they can give you better guidance in your relationship. It'll give your boyfriend/girlfriend a chance to see what you're like at home—how you treat your family, which will be some indication of how you are likely to treat any future family.

- Don't just give your friends and family the time you can't be together as a couple. Consciously decide not to see your boyfriend/girlfriend so that you can maintain these other relationships. Don't make your friends feel second best. Show how much you value and appreciate their friendship. Boy/girl relationships may end, but other friendships tend to endure.

- Work consciously at being together in a group without excluding others. Help each other develop better social skills. Don't keep making "in" jokes and exchanging meaningful glances as if you're communicating in a secret code. It's just rude, like whispering at the table.

- Enjoy your time with your friends! When you marry you (happily!) give up a certain amount of freedom to go out with friends, because

Make the most of being 'single'

your husband/wife becomes your first priority. It's wonderful, but it is restrictive. Make the most of being "single" (even if you're in a relationship). Don't make each other feel guilty about spending time with other friends—and this applies especially to friends of the opposite sex. It is important that both of you have friendships with both boys and girls.

An over-possessive boyfriend can make his girlfriend feel she can't ever talk to another guy, let alone be friends with him, and that's very unhealthy. He may say it's because he loves you so much, but what it really means is that he is insecure, and that he doesn't trust you to be able to talk to another male member of the species without falling in love with him! Of course, you both need to be sensitive to the other's feelings: if all your friends are guys, if you're spending lots of time with one particular fellow other than your boyfriend—if you seem to get on better with him, laugh uproariously at his jokes, share all kinds of experiences and secrets with him, then, of course, your boyfriend is going to feel left out and jealous (who wouldn't?). You need to talk openly and honestly, calmly and lovingly about these issues and make sure there is no misunderstanding.

Every stage of a relationship has its blessings. It may not always be easy to be content with where you're at, but you should ask God to give you grace to enjoy each stage as it comes. God has created us as many-dimensioned people and no one single human relationship, however wonderful, can answer all our needs. We need to cultivate and maintain all the relationships God gives us.

> **Winston, if I were married to you I'd put poison in your coffee.**
>
> **Nancy, if I were married to you I'd drink it.**

Lady Astor & Winston Churchill

CHAPTER SEVEN

where next?

If you wanted to make the journey from Belfast to New York, one of the least effective methods of travel would be to launch out on a raft in the vague hope that you would eventually drift there. Not many people choose a raft as their preferred means of crossing oceans, but it's amazing how many couples are happy to just drift along in their relationships and see where things take them.

How can you tell if your relationship is drifting? Re-examine the whole goal of going out—to find out whether you might be potential marriage partners. "Could we see ourselves as husband and wife?" Ask yourselves honestly if you are any closer to answering that crucial question today than you were this time a year ago. If the answer is no, then the chances are your relationship is drifting along aimlessly, without any clear goal. Going out isn't a game—your own feelings and someone else's are involved. Take it seriously. Don't just drift along from Friday night to Friday night without ever talking about the important issues of going out.

That brings us on to another danger in a drifting relationship—running away from conflict. No matter what kind of boat you're in, getting from Belfast to New York is not plain sailing. In any close relationship between two sinners who are communicating effectively there will inevitably be storms and, if you don't have a chart and are prepared to do some hard navigating, you will end up on the rocks. The longer two sinners go out, the more things each will discover about the other that annoys them. The better you get to know someone, the more likely you are to let your guard down and see one another as you really are. Now in a sense that's healthy, because obviously when you're married to someone you see them "warts and all". So the sooner you learn how to work through conflict and disagreement the better. And if you *can't* learn, or are unwilling to *try* to learn, the sooner you find that out the better.

Some couples proudly claim they never ever fight or disagree about anything. It may be that they simply don't know each other well enough yet, or aren't enough at ease with one another to say what they really think. Speaking personally, in the first six months of going out, we never disagreed about anything. We used to marvel at how "in tune" we were—how everything about the other person was so perfect. Sadly however, that perfect couple mysteriously disappeared after six months and has never been seen again! Or a couple may genuinely never disagree about anything, but the reason is that they never communicate properly. "A widow I know realised that the absence of conflict in her forty-year marriage had not necessarily been a good sign. 'I used to boast to friends about how well my husband and I got along,' she said, 'But now I see that part of the reason that we got along was because we never fought—and the reason we never fought was because we never really talked.'" (Joshua Harris, *Boy Meets Girl*)

Don't paper over the cracks. If you're serious, work hard… If you're not serious, end it now

Don't drift in your relationship. Don't run away from problems and conflict now just to keep the peace. Don't paper over the cracks. If you're serious about your relationship, work hard at dealing with these issues. If you're not serious, end it now. You're not being fair to the other person. Letting your relationship drift is a waste of time—you're monopolising your boyfriend's/girlfriend's affection and attention when it could be given to someone else who *is* serious.

Don't be surprised when conflict rears its ugly head in your relationship. You're both sinners—of course you're going to misunderstand each other, be insensitive to each other, hurt each other. Sin distorts and corrupts our ability to relate to one another as we should. So rather than hoping or trying to ensure that there will never be any conflict between you, accept that it's a sad reality of life in a fallen world and learn biblically how to deal with it. Approach conflict positively, as an opportunity to learn about each other, as a chance to practise forgiveness and reconciliation—two things Christians ought to know a

Know the difference between arguing and disagreeing

lot about. It's not easy or pleasant dealing with disagreements—it's far easier just to sweep the whole mess under a convenient carpet and go to the cinema, but your relationship will be much stronger after you've worked biblically through a problem together. Perhaps you think that's surprising. Some couples seem to think that, if they really love one another they will never quarrel or disagree about anything, and that, if they have an argument it means the relationship is over. In fact it's only really just beginning because you're getting past the stage of putting on your best face. What matters is not that you've had an argument, but how you deal with it. Please don't take us up wrongly here—we don't want to make it sound like a good relationship is a constant fight—far from it. Nor are we condoning or excusing couples who *are* constantly fighting. If your relationship is like that all the time, you should think long and hard about whether it has a future or not. But it is true that dealing with problems properly is a constructive, healthy and vital part of building a strong relationship.

Dealing with Conflict

Here are ten tips for communication that can help when you're experiencing conflict in your relationship. They're taken from a book called "Love That Lasts" by Gary and Betsy Ricucci. They won't make much sense if you just skim read them. We suggest that you take time to read and pray through them individually and as a couple and try to put them into practice—they are very practical and helpful principles:

1. Learn to express your feelings and frustrations honestly, but without accusing or attacking the other person (Proverbs 11.9).

2. Choose words, expressions and a tone of voice that are kind and gentle. Don't use speech that could easily offend or spark an argument (Proverbs 15.1).

3. Don't exaggerate, distort or stretch the truth. Avoid extreme words like *never* and *always* (Ephesians 4.25).

4. Give actual and specific examples. If necessary, make notes before you talk. Stay away from generalities (e.g. "You're just so selfish").

5. Commit yourself to seeking solutions instead of airing your grievances. Getting even isn't the goal—you want to get things resolved (Romans 12.17-21). It's not about winning an argument—it's about sorting out the root problems and moving forwards.

6. Listen to what the other person is saying, feeling and needing. Try to detect his or her underlying concerns (James 1.19).

7. Refuse to indulge bitterness, anger, withdrawal or argument. Though these emotions are normal, indulging them is sin (Ephesians 4.26).

8. Don't hesitate to acknowledge your own failure, and be quick to forgive the other person. Make sure you don't hold a grudge (Luke 17.3-4). N.B. Saying "I forgive you" means "I promise that I won't bring this up again or hold this against you." Don't say it lightly or falsely.

9. Keep talking and asking questions until you are sure that you both understand clearly what the other is saying and feeling. Encourage each other as you press toward a solution (Romans 14.19).

10. Train your mouth and heart until you can say the right thing at the right time in the right way for the right reasons.

"Make Your Mind Up Time"
If you're not just drifting in your relationship, but actively trying to steer a course through the obstacles towards the eventual goal of marriage, sooner or later you realise that you've reached the point where there really are only two options: to split up or to move towards engagement.

1. Splitting up
It may be that as time goes on you come to see that you're not right for each other. There are too many difficulties, differences and personality clashes. Perhaps your goals for your lives are incompatible. Recognise all of this as part of God's guidance. Be realistic. God guides us by sanctified common sense applied to our circumstances. How many more signs do you need that this relationship is not working?

> **Splitting up is not the end of the world... but marrying unwisely is a terrible mistake**

Splitting up doesn't mean that going out together was a mistake or a failure. Splitting up is not the end of the world. Remember the whole purpose of going out is to get to know one another and to explore together the possibility of marriage. If it becomes clear through going out that you're not right for each other then your relationship has served its purpose. It's a success! You may not have come to the conclusion you originally expected or hoped for. It may not be what your matchmaking friends wanted, but from the point of view of what's best for you, as far as your future happiness in concerned, it's a success. Marrying unwisely is a terrible mistake and Christians who do it have to bear the consequences of doing so "until death us do part."

There's a godly way to split up and an ungodly way

Splitting up in a Christian relationship, as in everything Christian, must be done very differently from the world, in love and with concern for the other person.

- This means being loving and sensitive in the way you break up. In the world often it's the case that each person wants to be the one who "dumps" the other. The very terms used by non-Christians for ending a relationship say it all: you "dump" or "chuck" someone like a piece of rubbish fit only for the bin; you "drop" them as if they have an infectious disease. Christians should never ever use that kind of language to describe breaking up with someone.

- Discuss breaking up properly and face to face. Don't send a note or a friend, followed by two years of not speaking to one another. Use this event to help one another grow in the Christian life. Splitting up for Christians should be a constructive thing: encourage one another; talk about each other's good qualities as well—don't just focus on all the frustrations and bad points; don't just criticise the other—acknowledge your own mistakes too.

- Work through it by yourselves as far as possible. If you need help, don't go to one of your friends who knows as much about relationships as you do! Go to an older and wiser couple, preferably your parents.

- Part on good terms. If you need to ask for forgiveness, do it. Don't drift afterwards into icy coldness, ignoring one another or treating each other like strangers. Stay friends, though at the same time be sensitive to how the other feels. One of you may be keen to spend quite a bit of time together, while the other may want a bit of distance.

- Don't give your friends a rerun of the whole "he said, she said" show. It's your business, no-one else's, so keep it to yourself. Do to others as you would have them do to you. If you wouldn't like your boyfriend to rehearse all the arguments and issues and problems to his mates, don't you do it to yours.

- Wait for a reasonable length of time before you go out with anyone else. It's the sensitive and the sensible thing to do. This includes getting back together with someone you've just split up with. It's not a good sign at all if a couple is going out one day, breaking up the next, going out again two days later, then breaking up again, etc, etc. It's a sign that they're not communicating properly. Even if you both feel you want to get back together again, give time to sort your feelings and thoughts out properly. There's nothing to lose by taking things slowly. If things were serious enough to break up in the first place, then those issues need to be resolved before you even think about going out again.

2. Getting engaged

Don't rush into engagement, even if things are going well and it's becoming more and more clear that you think you're right for each other. If you can't actually get married for another couple of years at least, we would urge you to wait. There is absolutely nothing to lose by waiting, but getting engaged too soon or being engaged for too long can cause problems.

If you get engaged too soon your relationship may not yet have been tested properly. Engagement isn't something to be entered into lightly. It's a solemn and public commitment—you're promising someone that you're going to marry them, and Christians keep their promises. We are to be people of our word—our "Yes" means yes, and our "No" no. That's not to say that engagement can't ever be broken off if someone is convinced they have made a mistake. It's always wrong to break your word, but it would be *more* wrong to marry foolishly.

If you're engaged for too long you open yourself up to greater sexual temptation

If you're engaged for too long you are opening yourself up to greater sexual temptation. Your sinful nature and the Devil will try to convince you that it's OK to go a little further now you're engaged. "You're going to get married after all. You've already made a public commitment to each other. We're practically husband and wife already…" and a thousand other lies. It's hard enough as it is to keep yourself pure over a lengthy relationship. Don't make it harder for yourselves.

So you're engaged?
Congratulations!! You've almost made it—well, sort of. You see this is just the end of the beginning. Your relationship is a dynamic thing—it carries on growing and changing. All you're doing now is entering into a new phase, one with its own challenges and joys. One of the most glorious, thrilling, exciting things about human relationships is that there are always new things to learn about one another, new dimensions of each other's character to discover. If it's allowed to go stale, if it's not nourished on a healthy diet of love and communication and self-giving, this relationship will wither and die. It takes work—that doesn't change after you get married. In many ways marriage

takes more work. Putting two sinners into the closest possible human relationship is bound to create some tensions. But by God's grace and in his strength and following his principles our relationships can be what he intends them to be, more and more. In our relationships, just as in every other aspect of human life, Romans 12.1-2 applies:

> "Therefore, I urge you, brothers, in view of God's mercy, to offer your bodies as living sacrifices, holy and pleasing to God—this is your spiritual act of worship. Do not conform any longer to the pattern of this world, but be transformed by the renewing of your mind. Then you will be able to test and approve what God's will is—His good, pleasing and perfect will."

APPENDIX

books

GOOD BOOKS TO READ ABOUT GOING OUT

Brian & Barbara Edwards, "No Longer Two" (Day One, 1994)

Joshua Harris, "I Kissed Dating Goodbye" (Multnomah, 1997)

Joshua Harris, "Boy Meets Girl" (Multnomah, 2000)

Joshua Harris, "Not Even a Hint" (Multnomah, 2003)

Josh McDowell, "Why Wait?" (Here's Life Publishers, 1987)

Linda Marshall, "Pure" (IVP, 2005)

Neil Richardson, "Courting Disaster" (Day One)

John White, "Eros Defiled" (IVP, 1977)